Masterpieces

Punctuation

LOWER JUNIOR

Charles Butchart and Sue Palmer

Content

Name ______________________________ Date ______________

Diagnostic assessment – Capital letters

Put **capital letters** in the right places in these sentences.

the dog was called spot.
my friend tom lives in america.
we go swimming every tuesday.

Set A
pages
3 - 4

All the **capital letters** are missing from this address.
Write it correctly on the envelope.

jack horner
3 pudding lane
plumsville
nr3 6tv

Set B
pages
5 - 6

Rewrite the following correctly, putting in the missing **capital letters**.

jack spratt would eat no fat,
his wife would eat no lean,
and so between the two of them
they licked the platter clean.

____
____
____
____

Set C
pages
7 - 8

vip stands for very important person.

____

mrs brown's favourite tv programme is neighbours.

____

Name ______________________________ Date ______________

Capital letters

Every sentence begins with a **capital letter**.

These are the **capital letters**.

A B C D E F G H I J K L M N O P Q R S T U V W X Y Z

1 Copy the **capital letters** here.

____

____

2 Fill in the missing **capital letters** in these sentences.

__he dog went for a walk.

__y dog is fat.

__e eats too much.

3 Write these words in the correct order to make sentences.

light us sun The gives

____

milk My cat likes

____

games enjoy We playing

____

Name ______________________ Date ______________

Capital letters

Proper nouns always begin with a **capital letter**.
The special names of people and animals are **proper nouns**.
The days of the week and months of the year are **proper nouns**.

Mrs Brown Sooty Anwar

1 Finish these sentences.

My teacher's name is ______________________

The boy in the picture is called ______________________

Mrs Brown's cat is called ______________________

2 Write these names correctly.

monday	____________	january	____________
friday	____________	october	____________
wednesday	____________	march	____________
sunday	____________	august	____________

3 Finish these sentences.

Today is ____________ *day. Yesterday was* ____________

The date today is ______________________

Name ______________________________ Date ______________

Capital letters

Every **sentence** begins with a **capital letter**.
Every **proper noun** begins with a **capital letter** –
The boy was called Jack and he lived in Birmingham.

1 Write these sentences correctly, putting in the **capital letters**.

the chang family are going to spain for their holiday.

____

in september leo and katy will both be nine.

____

In a **compound proper noun** each word begins with a capital letter – ***Q**ueen **V**ictoria*, ***M**anchester **U**nited*, ***H**igh **S**treet*.

2 Write these **compound proper nouns**, putting in the **capital letters**.

river thames ______________

new york ______________

bugs bunny ______________

3 Write these **sentences** correctly, putting in the **capital letters**.

sanjay's teacher is called mr jenkins.

____

the children are pupils at glen primary school.

____

in trafalgar square there are hundreds of pigeons.

____

Name ______________________ Date ____________

Capital letters

Every **sentence** begins with a **capital letter**.
Every **proper noun** begins with a **capital letter**.
In **compound proper nouns** each word begins with a **capital letter**.

1 Give the **proper nouns** in the picture their **capital letters**.

queen victoria

rudolf

eiffel tower

2 Now, write **sentences** to answer these questions.

Which reindeer had a red nose? ______________________

____

Who became queen in 1837? ______________________

____

Which famous tower is in Paris? ______________________

____

3 Write this name and address on the envelope, putting in **capital letters** where they are missed out.

wanda about
the hollies
mistletoe avenue
yule
y3 9ma

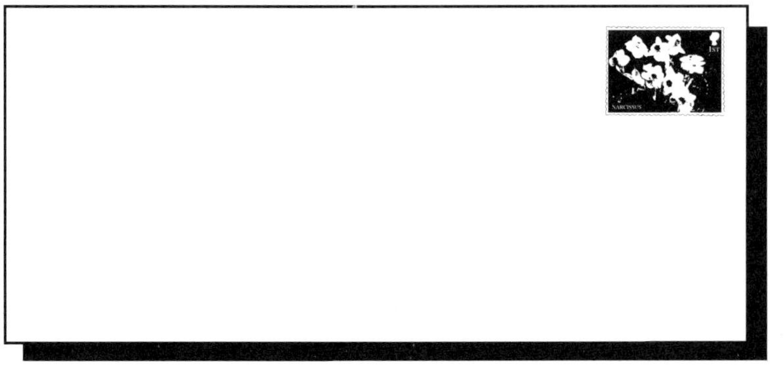

Name ______________________________ Date ______________

Capital letters

1 Correct this passage, putting **capital letters** at the beginnings of **sentences** and **proper nouns**.

florence nightingale was born in italy in 1820 and was named after the city of florence in which she was born. while she was still a girl, florence cared for sick animals and visited old people and invalids on her father's estate in derbyshire which was called lea hurst. when she was 18 years of age florence met queen victoria.

In poems and rhymes, each new line usually begins with a **capital letter**.

2 Write this rhyme, setting it out correctly. Put **capital letters** where they are needed.

little miss muffet sat on a tuffet eating her curds and whey. there came a big spider, who sat down beside her and frightened miss muffet away.

3 Choose a favourite rhyme or verse from a poem that you know by heart. Write it on the back of this sheet, setting it out correctly.

Name ______________________ Date ____________

Capital letters

Capital letters are often used in **abbreviations** – **BBC** for *British Broadcasting Corporation.*

1 Match these abbreviations to the words below.

PE MP PM PTO FA VIP TV USA EU UN

Football Association ______ Prime Minister ______

United States of America ______ television ______

very important person ______ physical education ______

please turn over ______ European Union ______

United Nations ______ Member of Parliament ______

2 a) Choose a passage from a book (about 100 words) with lots of **proper nouns** or **abbreviations** in it.
b) Write it out, missing out all the capital letters. Go on to the back of the sheet if necessary.
c) Give your passage to a friend to correct.
d) Then check in the book to see if your friend got it right.

Name ____________________ Date ____________

Diagnostic assessment – Full stops and sentences

Write the words in order to make **sentences**.
Give each sentence a **capital letter** and a **full stop**.

swimming ducks pond are the on the

____

winter is in cold the it

____

Set **A** pages 10 - 11

Write the **capital letters** and **full stops** in the correct places to make the number of **sentences** shown in brackets.

I like sweets my. Favourites are jelly babies. (2)

____

Our dog is. called Spot he is. a corgi he is two years old. (3)

____

Set **B** pages 12 - 13

Write two simple **sentences** about this picture.

____

____

____

____

Now, turn your two sentences into one sentence using a **conjunction**.

____

____

Set **C** pages 14 - 15

Name ______________________ Date ____________

Full stops and sentences

A **sentence** is a group of words that makes sense.
It begins with a **capital letter** and ends with a **full stop**.

1 Write these words in order so that they make sense and make a **sentence**.

the in birds morning the sing

____

up time is to get it

____

breakfast eat for toast we

____

2 Complete these **sentences**.

A sentence begins with a ____________ ____________ .

A sentence ends with a ____________ ____________ .

3 After each group of words write **'sentence'** or **'not a sentence'**.

the door knob not a sentence

the door knob is shiny ______________________

I turn the door knob ______________________

the old door ______________________

4 Give the **sentences** a **capital letter** and a **full stop**.

Name ______________________ Date ____________

Full stops and sentences

A **sentence** must make sense.

1 These groups of words do not make complete sense on their own. Match them up to form complete **sentences**.

the river bank	climbed out
my friend Peter	was slippery
the water in the river	was icy cold
Peter	fell in the river

2 Now, write the sentences using **capital letters** and **full stops**.

A group of words can make more than one **sentence**.

3 Read these words aloud. Put a **full stop** after each group that makes sense and makes a sentence. Remember **capital letters**.

I'm glad to meet you my name is Bill (2 sentences)

Fred worked hard in the garden the flowers are in bloom (2 sentences)

Name ______________________ Date ____________

Full stops and sentences

A **sentence** is a group of words that makes sense.
A **phrase** is part of a sentence. It might not need a capital letter or full stop.

1 Write **phrase** or **sentence** after each group of words. Put a **capital letter** at the beginning of the **sentences** and a **full stop** at the end.

the big, ginger cat ________ a car raced past ________

the silver moon ________ the light flickered ________

2 Write a **phrase** about this picture. Then write a **sentence** about it.

____

____

3 In these **sentences,** the **capital letters** and **full stops** are in the wrong places. Write them correctly to make the number of **sentences** shown in brackets.

The alien is green his name is. Foz he has two heads. (3)

____

Foz is visiting Earth for. A week it is his summer holiday. (2)

____

Name ______________________ Date ____________

Full stops and sentences

1 Answer each question with a **sentence**. Remember **capital letters** and **full stops**.

What is your favourite colour?

My favourite colour is green.

What is your favourite subject at school?

____

What do you like doing in your spare time?

____

2 Answer these questions in **sentences**.

Why do we have to go to school?

____

What makes you feel excited?

____

Simple sentences can be joined by **conjunctions** to make one **sentence**.
because · so · when

3 Choose the best **conjunction** to join these pairs of **sentences**.

The children jumped for joy. It was time to go home.

The children jumped for joy when it was time to go home.

The baby wanted its mother. It began to cry.

____

The headmaster looked stern. The children were rather noisy.

____

Name ________________________ Date ____________

Full stops and sentences

Sentences are groups of words that **make sense**.
Simple **sentences** can be joined together to make longer **sentences** using **conjunctions**.

1 Correct these examples by making them into two **sentences**, using **full stops** and **capital letters**.

A flying saucer landed on Mary's front lawn she was alarmed.

A hatch slowly opened after a few moments a green head appeared.

Mary's dog gave a sudden, sharp bark the head withdrew at once.

The craft spun off into the distance had Skipper saved the world?

2 Choose a **conjunction** to make a longer sentence from each of these pairs of simple sentences.

because	so	when

Mr Brown was pleased. The class had worked well.

____

The bags were full of gold. The mean old man gleefully rubbed his hands.

____

____

Milly's new hat was whipped off her head. There was a sudden gust of wind.

____

____

Name ________________________ Date ____________

Full stops and sentences

1 Write a **paragraph** of about eight sentences all about a birthday party (real or imaginary). Check your **punctuation** with your teacher.

2 a) Rewrite your **paragraph** on a separate piece of paper, leaving out all the full stops and capital letters.
b) Give it to your friend to correct by putting in the missing punctuation.
c) Check it together using your **paragraph** above and see if you agree.

3 Use **conjunctions** to link some of the simple sentences in the paragraph below so that it makes sense.

The children were bored. They had nothing to do. They decided to go swimming. They asked their parents. They got there. They were disappointed to find the pool closed. It was being repaired. A serious leak had been discovered. They were amused. They thought about it. A pool without water would be a pit!

Name ______________________ Date ____________

Diagnostic assessment – Question marks and exclamation marks

Write the word **statement** or **question** after each sentence. Put **full stops** or **question marks** at the ends of the sentences.

Set A
pages 17 - 18

What is your name ______________________

My dog is called Rover ______________________

How old is he ______________________

Write down an **exclamation** that you might make in these events. The first one is done for you.

Set B
pages 19 - 20

You are falling off a boat. Help, I'm falling!

You see a beautiful sunset. ______________________

Your dog is running away. ______________________

Write another short sentence for each of these characters. Connie makes **statements**, Tim asks **questions** and Edward **exclaims**.

Confident Connie   Timid Tim   Exclaiming Edward

Set C
pages 21 - 22

Name ______________________________ Date ______________

Question marks

A **question** is a special kind of **sentence**. It ends with **?** – a question mark.

1 Put these words in order to make **question** sentences. Remember **capital letters** and **question marks**.

may play you with I ______________________________

door the shall I close ______________________________

crying you are why ______________________________

who porridge ate my ______________________________

2 Put in **capital letters** and **question marks**. Then write the **answers** to the **questions**. The first one has been started for you.

What day is it today? Today is Wednesday.

how old are you ______________________________

what is your teacher's name ______________________________

is it spring, summer or autumn ______________________________

3 Write three **questions** you could ask about the man in the picture.

____

____

____

____

____

____

Name ______________________ Date ____________

Question marks and exclamation marks

A **statement** ends with a **full stop**.
A **question** ends with a **question mark**.
An **exclamation** ends with an **exclamation** mark.

1 Write either **statement** or **question** after each sentence. Then put either **full stops** or **question marks** at the ends.

Do you eat peas with your knife ____________

I eat peas with my knife ____________

Will you be long ____________

I hope you won't be long ____________

2 Put **exclamation marks** after these exclamations.

It's horrible

I can't bear it

What a monster

Help me

Save us

Stay away

3 Write **exclamations** that might be made when –

You win a raffle.

____

You lose a pound coin.

____

You see a ghost.

____

Your friend is in danger.

____

Name ______________________ Date ____________

Question marks

1 Write either **statement** or **question** after these sentences. Put **question marks** after the sentences that are questions and **full stops** after the statements.

Will you be long in the bathroom ____________

I must have a shower before breakfast ____________

There is a queue out here ____________

Shall we break the door down ____________

2 These sentences are either **statements** or **questions**. Rewrite them and put in the correct punctuation.

Where does milk come from ____________

Butter is made from cream ____________

Do you prefer butter or margarine ____________

____

3 These **statements** are **answers**. Write the **questions** that might have been asked.

Question: ____________

Answer: We went to France for our holiday.

Question: ____________

Answer: It was sunny most of the time but we had two days of rain.

Name ______________________________ Date ______________

Question marks and exclamation marks

An **exclamation mark** shows that a sentence is meant to be said in an urgent way or not taken too seriously.

1 Write an **exclamation** that you might make in these events. The first is done for you.

Your foot is caught in a grid. Help, I'm stuck!

Smoke is coming from a building. ______________

You want to keep something secret. ______________

2 Change these **statements** to **exclamations**. The first has been done for you.

It is very wet today. What a wet day!

I think your trainers are great. ______________

This is a delicious pudding. ______________

3 Put a **full stop**, **question mark** or **exclamation mark** to finish each speech in this play. Add some more speeches. Go on to the back of the sheet if you need to.

Anwar: Remember your boots

Joel: Oh dear, I forgot them

Bryn: You can borrow my spares

Joel: Do you think they'll fit me

Bryn: ______________

Anwar: ______________

Name ______________________ Date ____________

Question marks and exclamation marks

Punctuation helps to give our writing the expression of spoken language.
A **statement** ends with a **full stop**.
A **question** ends with a **question mark**.
An **exclamation** ends with an **exclamation mark**.

1 Rewrite these sentences in the appropriate column and punctuate them correctly. Add one example of your own to each column.

Listen to me We shall visit them How do you know

Statement	Question	Exclamation

2 Write another short sentence for each of these characters. Connie makes statements, Tim asks questions and Edward exclaims.

Confident Connie

Timid Tim

Exclaiming Edward

3 Use punctuation to turn this text into different kinds of sentences – statements, questions and exclamations.

I wonder what lies behind that mysterious old door there's only one way to find out I shall open it here goes I can hardly turn the key the lock must be rusty should I have another go this time I shall use both hands I think it's turning oh no the key has broken off now I'll never know

Name ______________________ Date ____________

Question marks and exclamation marks

1 a) Imagine you are thinking aloud about choosing a present for a friend. Write down your thoughts. Include **statements**, **questions** and **exclamations**.

b) Rewrite the text on a separate piece of paper, leaving out all the punctuation marks.

c) Ask your friend to put in the punctuation. Compare your friend's version with your own. Which seems best?

2 Complete this scene from a play, including **statements**, **questions** and **exclamations**. Introduce more characters. Continue on the back of this sheet if you need to.

King:	*We must prepare for battle.*
Red Knight:	*But, Sire, are our men prepared?*
Black Knight:	*I'm always ready!*

Name ______________________ Date ____________

Diagnostic assessment – Commas

Finish these lists. Don't forget the **commas**.

The days of the week are Monday, Tuesday

____

The months of the year are January, February, March

____

____

The colours of the rainbow are ______________________

____

Set A
pages 24 - 25

Write **,** or **•** in the boxes.

Long ☐ long ago ☐ dinosaurs ruled the world ☐

Feeling very tired and hungry ☐ the lost dog slumped in a corner ☐

Welcome to our school ☐ It is over 100 years old ☐

Set B
pages 26 - 27

Use **commas** to punctuate this sentence in three different ways. Make the shop sell 3 things, 4 things and 5 things.

3 things: The shop sold silver candlesticks gold watches and jewellery.

4 things: The shop sold silver candlesticks gold watches and jewellery.

5 things: The shop sold silver candlesticks gold watches and jewellery.

Set C
pages 28 - 29

Name ______________________________ Date ______________

Commas

A **comma** looks like a full stop with a little tail. The tail goes below the line. We use **commas** to separate the items in a list – *We bought butter, cheese, eggs and milk at the shop*. You do not usually need a comma before *and*.

1 Practise writing commas here.

, , ____

2 Put **commas** to separate the items in these lists.

Jake's four best friends are Baz Mel Tina and Aziz.

His four favourite foods are chicken pizza chapati and chips.

The foods Jake hates most are peas burgers icecream and spinach.

3 Finish these lists. Don't forget the **commas**.

My four best friends are ______________________________

____

My four favourite foods are ____________________________

____

The four foods I hate most are __________________________

____

Name ______________________ Date ______________

Commas and full stops

A **comma** can show a very short break for breath inside a sentence. A **comma** can *never* finish a sentence.

1 Put **,** or **.** in the squares.

Without looking back ☐ the boy set off down the road ☐

Every Wednesday ☐ my brother goes to scouts ☐

Looking like a beautiful princess ☐ Cinderella came into the ballroom ☐

2 Go over the **commas** to make them stand out, then finish each of these **sentences**.

When I get up in the morning, I ______________________

Long, long ago, there were ______________________

If our teacher is angry, ______________________

3 Read these groups of words. Write **,** or **.** in the squares.

It's nice to meet you ☐ I'm called Pradeep ☐

Whenever I get the chance ☐ I go to the library ☐

Reading is my hobby ☐ I get a new book out every week ☐

If I can find any ☐ I get books on football for my friend ☐

Whether it's reading or football ☐ everybody needs a hobby ☐

Name ______________________________ Date ______________

Commas

We use **commas** to separate the items in a list – *For the picnic we packed crisps, boiled eggs, ham sandwiches and cans of drink.*
We do not usually put a **comma** before *and*.

1 Put **commas** to separate the items in these lists.

To finish my picture I need light blue dark red and bright yellow crayons.

Iqbal's favourite TV soaps are Neighbours Eastenders Coronation Street and Emmerdale.

For his birthday Jake wanted a new football some trainers a computer game and a Roald Dahl book.

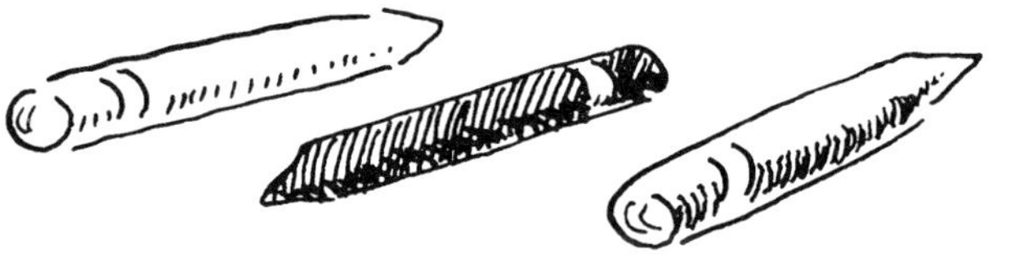

2 Finish these lists. Don't forget the **commas**.

My four favourite pop groups are ______________________________

____

Four British cities are ______________________________

____

Three European countries are ______________________________

____

3 Put **commas** to separate the items in the lists in these sentences.

Lassie the dog Fluffy the cat and Bobs the budgie all live with old Mrs Wilks.

Alana has black hair brown eyes long dark eyelashes and beautiful skin.

Name ______________________ Date ______________

Commas and full stops

1 Some of these groups of words do not make sense on their own. Match them up to form complete **sentences**.

Very softly,	the piper danced into town.
I'm coming to find you,	Goldilocks crept into the cottage.
Wearing a strange coat of many colours,	ready or not.

2 Write out the **sentences** from Question 1. Don't forget **commas** and **full stops**.

____

____

____

____

3 Read these groups of words. Put , or • in the squares. (If you choose a full stop, make sure the next sentence starts with a capital letter.)

Once upon a time ☐ there was a wicked witch ☐

She lived in a cottage in the wood ☐ far from the village ☐

Her cat lived with her ☐ Her cat was called Fizz ☐

Even though he was a witch's cat ☐ Fizz didn't like magic ☐

Whenever the witch did a spell ☐ Fizz sneaked outside ☐

He hated the smell of magic ☐ it made him feel sick ☐

Name ______________________ Date ____________

Commas

We use **commas** to separate the items in a list. Sometimes these items consist of several words.

1 Use **commas** to separate the items in these sentences.

Jo's baby sister sleeps in a cot wears a nappy drinks from a baby's bottle and eats babies porridge from a spoon.

When Kumar gets up in the morning he cleans his teeth washes his face gets dressed and goes down for breakfast.

At school we do sums in Maths lessons writing in English lessons painting in Art lessons and lots of other things.

2 Finish these sentences, using lists of at least three things each time. Don't forget the **commas**.

If I had three wishes I'd wish for ______________________

____

The best things about my best friend are ______________________

____

The most exciting things I've ever done are ______________________

____

3 Use **commas** to punctuate this sentence three different ways. Make the monster eat three things, four things or five things.

The monster liked to eat metal polish plastic bags and Weetabix. (3)

The monster liked to eat metal polish plastic bags and Weetabix. (4)

The monster liked to eat metal polish plastic bags and Weetabix. (5)

Name ______________________ Date ____________

Commas and full stops

A **comma** shows a short break for breath in the middle of a sentence.
A **full stop** shows the end of a sentence.

1 Use one **comma** and one **full stop** to punctuate each of these **sentences**.

Wearing a false beard and a pair of dark glasses the detective slunk along the street

Thousands of miles away on the other side of the world everyone is tucked up and fast asleep in bed

Not wishing to be rude Amy said nothing about Alice's hat

2 Put a **comma** after each of the **phrases** below and write an ending for the sentence.

At three thirty every Friday afternoon ______________________

____

With a cheerful grin ______________________

____

After a long day at school ______________________

____

By the end of the summer holidays ______________________

____

3 Write this passage on the back of this sheet, putting in **commas**, **full stops** and **capital letters**.

martin can eat anything whatever sort of food you put in front of him martin will manage to finish it he gobbles down fruit fish meat vegetables and dairy products he eats sweet foods salty foods and sour foods he swallows it all down so fast that sometimes I think he doesn't even taste it known to his friends as the human dustbin martin is definitely the world's best eater

Name ______________________ Date ____________

Diagnostic assessment – Direct speech

Write the correct **direct speech** in each space.

"_______________________!"
cried the swimmer.

The newsreader said
"_______________________."

Set A
pages
31 - 32

Read this story, then underline the **direct speech** in red and put speech marks round all the **direct speech**.

What's for dinner? asked Rosie.

Chicken and salad, replied her mother.

Why can't we have sausages? Rosie asked.

Sausages aren't very good for you, her mother said.

Yes, but they taste nice! said Rosie.

Set B
pages
33 - 34

Write a sentence containing **direct speech** to answer these questions.

"What happened to Humpty Dumpty?" asked the king.

____

"Who are you?" asked Little Miss Muffet.

____

Set C
pages
35 - 36

Name ______________________ Date ______________

Direct speech

The words in **speech marks** are called **direct speech**.
We start a new line whenever a new speaker begins to speak.

1 Who is speaking in these sentences?

The doctor asked, "How are you today?" the doctor

"Pass the ball!" called Sam. ______________

Miss Thorpe told the class, "Do your best." ______________

2 Look at the pictures and write the **correct direct** speech in each space.

Umer called, "______________________________________"

The postman said, "__________________________________"

3 Copy this out, starting a new line whenever you need to.

Mum called, "Are you coming?" "I'm not ready yet," said Jo. "How long will you be?" asked Mum. "Only five more minutes," answered Jo.

____

____

____

____

Name ______________________ Date ______________

Direct speech

The words in speech marks are called **direct speech**.
In **direct speech**, we start a **new line** for each **new speaker**.

1 Write the **direct speech** in the correct speech bubbles.

The singer said, "I am nervous."

"Where are you going?" the policeman asked.

"I forgot my football boots," cried Jess.

2 Write the words in the speech bubbles as **direct speech**.
Start a new line whenever you need to.

" ______________________ " asked Idi.

Emma replied, " ______________________ "

" ______________________ " asked Idi.

Emma said, " ______________________ "

Name ______________________ Date ____________

Direct speech

> The words in **speech marks** are called **direct speech**.
> The words that tell you who's speaking are called the **reporting clause**.

1 Underline the **direct speech** in blue and the **reporting clause** in red.

"We are going to the beach," said Mr Cox.

"Why are you wearing dark glasses?" Saida asked.

Mr Cox explained, "The sunshine hurts my eyes."

"Now we don't know who you are looking at," said the children.

2 Complete the sentences by writing in either the correct **direct speech** or **reporting clause**.

Do your best	*said the doctor*	*called Tanya*	*Open your mouth wide*

"I hope you feel better," ______________

"______________," Mrs Watson told the class.

"Pass the ball to me," ______________

"______________," said the dentist.

3 Read this story, then underline the **direct speech** in blue and the **reporting clauses** in red. Put **speech marks** round all the direct speech.

We did an exam at school today, said Alice.

Her mum asked, Did you enjoy it?

Not at all, answered Alice.

Oh dear. Did you have trouble with some of the questions? asked her mum.

No, but I had trouble with some of the answers! said Alice.

Name ______________________________ Date ______________

Direct speech

There is always a punctuation mark between the **direct speech** and the **reporting clause**.
It can be a **question mark** or an **exclamation mark** but not a **full stop**. Usually it is a **comma**.

1 Choose the best punctuation mark to put in the box. **! ? ,**

"I feel very nervous☐" said the singer.

"Where are you going☐" asked the policeman.

"Pass my glasses☐" called Grandpa.

The captain shouted☐"Ship ahoy!"

Mother said☐"I want you to come straight home."

"How old are you☐" asked Jess.

"I'm going to win this contest☐" roared the wrestler.

2 Rewrite this play as **direct speech**. Put in **reporting clauses**. Put in the speech marks and any other punctuation you need.

Policeman:	What are you up to?
Burglar Bill:	Just looking at the stars.
Policeman:	Then why do you need a ladder?
Burglar Bill:	To get a closer look!

____

____

____

____

Name ______________________ Date ____________

Direct speech

1 Punctuate the **direct speech**. Give the first word spoken a **capital letter**. Put correct punctuation between the **direct speech** and the **reporting clause**. Put **speech marks** round the **direct speech**.

what game shall we play asked Henry

Hamish replied let's play rounders

the grass has been cut exclaimed Hannah

well let's choose teams suggested Hugo

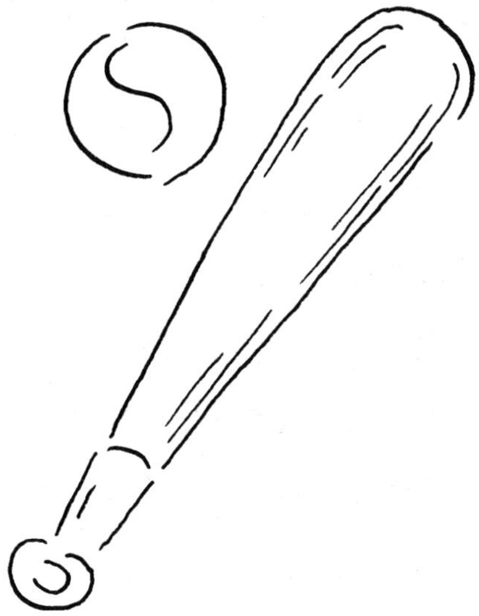

2 Write a sentence containing **direct speech** to answer these questions. The first one has been done for you.

John suggested, "Shall we build a treehouse?"

"What a good idea," replied Mai Ling.

"Would you like to go on a mystery tour?" the driver asked.

____

The doctor enquired, "How are you feeling today?"

____

"How are you today, Grandma?" asked Red Riding Hood.

____

"Who is the fairest of them all?" enquired the wicked queen.

____

"Do you know the answer?" whispered Jason.

____

Name ______________________ Date ____________

Direct speech

1 Rewrite this passage setting out the **direct speech** correctly. Remember to begin a **new line** for each new speaker. Add all the necessary punctuation.

Ged was sitting thinking in his garden when he heard a strange, squeaky voice. Help me someone called. I can't see anybody said Ged to himself. Please, help me cried the invisible person. This is very mysterious said Ged to himself. He could still see no one, even after looking round. Please, come and help me, called the voice even more urgently. Ged walked slowly round the garden and caught sight of the garden gnome lying on his back behind some flower pots. Surely not he muttered. But sure enough the fat, little gnome called again please help me. How would you like to be lying on your back and unable to get up!

Name ______________________ Date ______________

Diagnostic assessment – Apostrophes in contractions

1 Change these words to **contractions**.
Put a ring round the letter that is missed out.

Set A
pages 38 - 39

is n(o)t isn't

we are ______

have not ______

they are ______

must not ______

it is ______

2 Correct these mistakes.

Set B
pages 40 - 41

might of X ______

are'nt X ______

would of X ______

were'nt X ______

must of X ______

isent X ______

3 Rewrite these sentences, changing all the **contractions** into **complete words**.

Set C
pages 42 - 43

We'll be setting off at four o'clock.
It's a dark night, and we don't know the way.
'Tis late, and we're far from home.

______

______

______

Name ______________________ Date ____________

Apostrophes in contractions

> Two words put together are often shortened by missing out letters.
> An **apostrophe** shows where letters are missing.

1 Match the **contractions** to the **complete words**.

I'm	is not
hadn't	have not
isn't	I am
aren't	had not
haven't	does not
doesn't	are not

2 Write the two words that these **contractions** stand for.

can't	can not	haven't	________
hadn't	________	didn't	________
mustn't	________	doesn't	________

3 Change these words to **contractions**.

were not	weren't	have not	________
has not	________	are not	________
is not	________	can not	________

4 Make **contractions** from these words. Put a ring round the letter that is missed out.

I(a)m	I'm	she is	________
you are	________	we are	________
he is	________	they are	________

Name ______________________ Date ____________

Apostrophes in contractions

1 Put a ring round the letters that are missed out when **contractions** are made from these words.

I have – I've	he has – he's	I had – I'd
you have – you've	she has – she's	you had – you'd
they have – they've	it has – it's	we had – we'd

2 Change these pairs of words to **contractions**.

I shall	I'll	they will	________
we shall	________	we will	________
it will	________	you will	________

3 Change these **contractions** to complete words.

I've ____I have____

you've ________________

he's ________________

she's ________________

I'd ________________

you'd ________________

4 Rewrite this sentence. Change the words that are underlined to **contractions**.

I will give you a bike when you have learned the rules of the road.

____

____

Name ______________________ Date ____________

Apostrophes in contractions

The **apostrophe** shows where letters are missing.

1 Change these **contractions** to complete words.

hadn't	________	don't	________
hasn't	________	doesn't	________
haven't	________	won't	________

2 Form **contractions** from these pairs of words.

I have	________	it has	________	I had	________
you have	________	she has	________	you had	________
we have	________	he has	________	they had	________

3 The **apostrophe** is in the wrong place in each of these words. Write the complete words. Put a ring round the letters that should be missed out. Write the **contraction** correctly.

are'nt ✗	are not ✓	aren't ✓
were'nt ✗	________	________
was'nt	________	________
is'nt ✗	________	________

4 Rewrite these sentences. Change the words that are underlined to **contractions**.

<u>You have</u> had a tiring day so <u>you had</u> better go to bed early.

____

<u>They will</u> have to play well if <u>they are</u> going to win the match.

____

Name ______________________ Date ____________

Apostrophes in contractions

1 Make **contractions** from these complete words.

could not couldn't
cannot ____________
will not ____________
must not ____________
might not ____________

2 Write the complete words that these **contractions** stand for.

I've ____________
we've ____________
you've ____________
they've ____________
could've ____________
would've ____________
should've ____________
might've ____________

3 Correct these mistakes.

might of ✗ might have or might've ✓
must of ✗ ____________
should of ✗ ____________
would of ✗ ____________
could of ✗ ____________
isent ✗ ____________
dosent ✗ ____________
wasent ✗ ____________

Name ______________________ Date ____________

Apostrophes in contractions

1 Rewrite the sentences, changing the **contractions** for complete words.

She should've remembered to bring her guitar.

____

The star singer mightn't turn up for the concert.

____

Their means belonging to them. **They're** means they are. **There** is a place word.

2 Use **their**, **they're** or **there** to fill the spaces in these sentences.

Many children have forgotten to bring __________ dinner money.
__________ supposed to bring it on Mondays.
They usually put it on the table over __________ .

Now, write some sentences of your own using **their**, **they're** or **there**.

____

____

____

Its means **belonging to it**. **It's** means **it is** or **it has**.

3 Use either **its** or **it's** to fill the spaces in these sentences.

The snail carries __________ house on __________ back.
__________ a lot for a small chap to carry.

Now, write sentences of your own using **its** and **it's**.

____

____

Name ______________________________ Date ______________

Apostrophes in contractions

Contractions are often used in poetry, texts from the past and in writing dialect forms of English.

1 Match the **contractions** with the correct complete words.

e'en	of the clock
o'clock	violoncello
'tis	evening
'cello	ever
'twas	it is
e'er	it was

2 Rewrite these lines of poetry changing the **contractions** to complete words.

'Tis the voice of the Lobster: I heard him declare...

____

I told you before 'twas a stormy night...

____

And when I see thee hang thy head, 'twill be my turn to watch thy bed...

____

____

3 This Scottish poem is about dawn and the first light of the day. Rewrite it using standard English words in place of the dialect **contractions**.

Wee Davie Daylicht keeks owre the sea,
Early in the mornin', wi' a clear e'e;
Waukens a' the birdies that are sleepin' soun',
Wee Davie Daylicht is nae lazy loon.

____

____

____

____

Name ______________________ Date ______________

Diagnostic assessment – Apostrophes and possession

Look at the pictures. Who are the owners and what do they own?

the fairy's wand — The fairy owns the wand.

Naseem's book — ______________________

Set A
pages 45 - 46

Rewrite these sentences using **apostrophe + s phrases** instead of the underlined ones.

The book belonging to Richard is very exciting.

____

The chair belonging to the dentist goes up and down.

____

The trunk belonging to the elephant was very long.

____

Set B
pages 47 - 48

Rewrite these sentences using **apostrophe phrases** instead of the underlined ones.

The cat belonging to the lady was black.

____

The cat belonging to the princess was white.

____

We saw the dog belonging to the little princesses on TV.

____

Set C
pages 49 - 50

Name ______________________ Date ____________

Apostrophes and possession

An **apostrophe + s** shows ownership.

1 Who is the owner?

the nest belonging to the bird ___the bird___

the crown belonging to the king ____________

the spade belonging to the gardener ____________

2 Who is the owner?

the cat's whiskers ___the cat___

Ali's football ____________

the cow's horns ____________

3 Who are the owners and what do they own?

the baby's pram ___The baby owns the pram.___

the clown's nose ____________

the referee's whistle ____________

Name ______________________ Date __________

Apostrophes and possession

An **apostrophe + s** shows ownership.

1 Complete the exercise.

John's coat

the coat belonging to John

the giant's castle

____

the judge's wig

____

2 Show ownership by using **apostrophe + s phrases**.

the horse belonging to Alexander Alexander's horse

the ship belonging to the pirate ______________________

the armour belonging to the knight ______________________

3 Show ownership by using **apostrophe + s phrases**.

<u>The glasses belonging to Grandma</u> are broken.

____

<u>The team belonging to Anwar</u> won the game.

____

Name ______________________ Date ____________

Apostrophes and possession

An **apostrophe + s** shows ownership.

1 Complete this exercise.

Kate's friend — the friend belonging to Kate
the referee's whistle ______________________
Hamish's dog ______________________
the postman's van ______________________

2 Show ownership by using **apostrophe + s phrases**.

the computer belonging to Class 9 — Class 9's computer
the pen belonging to Mr Cook ______________________
the kittens belonging to the cat ______________________
the mast belonging to the ship ______________________

3 Rewrite these sentences using **apostrophe + s phrases** to show ownership instead of the words underlined.

<u>The horns belonging to the bull</u> were massive.
The bull's horns were massive.

<u>The car belonging to the Queen</u> drew up.
____

<u>The rod belonging to the fisherman</u> snapped.
____

<u>The field belonging to the farmer</u> was muddy.
____

Name ______________________ Date ____________

Apostrophes and possession

1 Circle the unwanted apostrophe in these phrases. Write each phrase in full.

the animal's track's — the tracks belonging to the animal

the artist's painting's ____________

the boy's sister's ____________

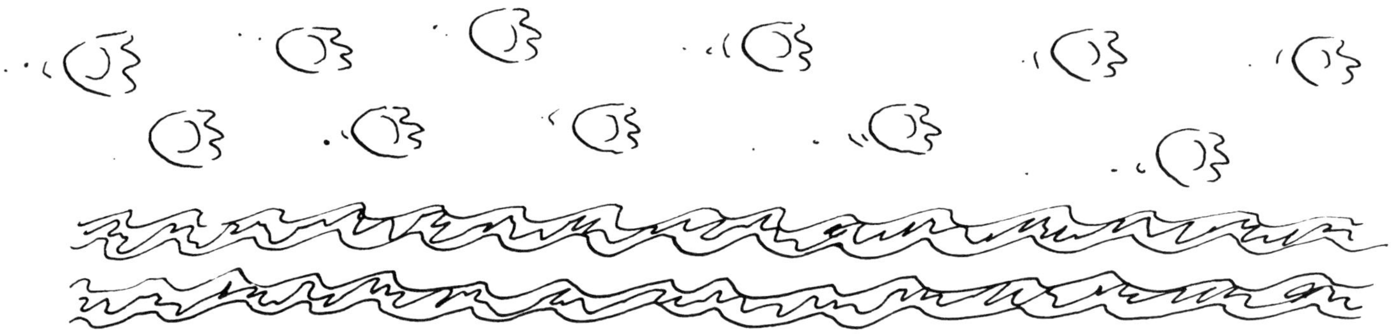

2 Put a line under the owner and circle the unwanted apostrophes. Then rewrite the sentences correctly.

After game's <u>Ted</u>'s shoe's were missing.

After games Ted's shoes were missing.

The van's tyre's had left a pattern in the snow.

____

The farmer's potatoe's were stored in sack's.

____

3 Rewrite this paragraph using **apostrophe + s phrases** instead of the words underlined.

We were at <u>the house belonging to Umer</u>. He was <u>the cousin belonging to Rosie</u>. We were listening to music in <u>the bedroom belonging to Umer</u>.

____

____

Name ______________________ Date ____________

Apostrophes and possession

Plural nouns usually end in **s**. To show ownership, we put an **apostrophe** after the **s** – *The boys' cloakroom.*

1 Rewrite these phrases using **apostrophes** to show ownership.

the barking belonging to the dogs — the dogs' barking

the crying belonging to the babies ____________

the laughter belonging to the girls ____________

2 Rewrite these phrases like the example.

the trees' leaves — the leaves belonging to the trees

the boys' boots ____________

the horses' stables ____________

the frogs' spawn ____________

3 Rewrite this passage using **apostrophe phrases** instead of the words underlined.

Class 6 made a plan to tidy up <u>the cloakroom belonging to the pupils</u>. They decided that <u>the coats and PE kit belonging to the boys</u> would be hung on the right. Then there would be space for <u>the things belonging to the girls</u> to go on the left. The teacher praised <u>the plan belonging to the pupils</u>.

____

____

____

____

____

____

Name ______________________________ Date ______________

Apostrophes and possession

1 Write the phrases. The first one is done for you.

the princess's clothes the clothes belonging to the princess

the princesses' clothes ______________________________

the witch's spells ______________________________

2 Rewrite these sentences using **apostrophe phrases** to show ownership.

The judge said the court should hear the evidence belonging to the witness.

____

There were drinks and sandwiches on the trolleys belonging to the stewardesses.

____

____

3 Rewrite this paragraph and put the **apostrophes** either before or after the **s** to show ownership. Write on the back if you need to.

The flag was flying over the kings castle. The queens daughters were arguing. It was the choice of the princesses husbands that was causing trouble. If only the duchesses sons had all been clever and handsome the princesses problems would have been solved!

____

____

____

____

____

____

Name ______________________ Date ____________

Diagnostic assessment – Revision

Put in all the capital letters and write the correct punctuation mark in each box.

Choose from **. ? ! '**

Biff my dog hasn☐t got a nose☐
Bessie how does he smell☐
Biff terrible☐

Set A pages 52 - 55

Put in all the capital letters and write the correct punctuation mark in each box.

Choose from **. ? ! , ' " "**

when goldilocks was walking in the forest she found a little cottage and looked inside☐on the table were three bowls of porridge☐there was a big bowl☐a medium-sized bowl and a little bowl☐the little girl☐s mouth watered☐
☐i☐d love a taste of porridge☐☐she said☐

Set B pages 56 - 59

Rewrite this passage correctly, putting in all the missing capital letters and punctuation marks. Start a new line when necessary.

doctor doctor my wife thinks she s a swallow said mr brown oh dear why can t mrs brown come and see me herself asked the doctor she s flown south for the winter replied mr brown

____

____

____

____

Set C pages 60 - 64

Name ______________________ Date __________

Revision

1 Using coloured pens, write over the punctuation below:
a) **capital letters** in red
b) **full stops, question marks** and **exclamation marks** in blue
c) **commas** and **apostrophes** in green.

Biff	Knock, knock.
Bessy	Who's there?
Biff	Ivor.
Bessy	Ivor who?
Biff	Ivor you open this door or I knock it down!

Patient	Doctor, doctor, I think I'm a bridge.
Doctor	Now then, what's come over you?
Patient	So far, three cars and a bus.

2 In the jokes below, the boxes show where punctuation marks have been missed out. Write the correct **punctuation mark** in each box. Put in all the **capital letters**.

Biff	knock □ knock □
Bessy	who □ s there □
Biff	harry □
Bessy	harry who □
Biff	harry up and open this door □

Patient	doctor □ doctor □ I think I □ m a pair of curtains □
Doctor	now then □ why should you think that □
Patient	people keep telling me to pull myself together □

Name ____________________ Date ____________

Revision

1 In the jokes below the boxes show where punctuation marks have been missed out. Write the correct **punctuation mark** in each box. Put in all the **capital letters.**

Biff	knock ☐ knock ☐
Bessy	who ☐ s there ☐
Biff	twitter ☐
Bessy	twitter who ☐
Biff	I didn't know you did owl impressions ☐

Patient	doctor ☐ doctor ☐ I think I can see into the future ☐
Doctor	when did this start ☐
Patient	next Wednesday ☐

2 Write out this joke again, putting in all the **capital letters** and the **punctuation marks** (where there are circles).

tammy	please can I have some apples ○ some grapes ○ some bananas and three wasps ○
greengrocer	we don ○ t sell wasps here ○
tammy	then why do you have some in your shop window ○

____

____

____

____

____

Name ______________________________ Date ______________

Revision

1 Using coloured pens, write over the punctuation below:
a) **capital letters** in red
b) **full stops, question marks** and **exclamation marks** in blue
c) **speech marks**, **commas** and **apostrophes** in green.

"Knock, knock," said Biff.
"Who's there?" asked Bessie, wearily.
"Isobel," answered Biff.
Bessie asked, "Isobel who?"
"Isobel not better than all this knocking?" said Biff.
"Ha ha ha!" laughed Bessie.

The patient said, "Doctor, doctor, I think I've got water on the knee."
"Oh well, I'll give you a tap on the ankle," said the doctor.

2 In the jokes below the boxes show where punctuation marks have been missed out. Write the correct **punctuation mark** in each box. Put in all the **capital letters**.

□ knock □ knock □ □ said biff □
□ who □ s there □ □ asked bessie □ smiling □
□ wendy □ □ answered biff □
bessie asked □ □ wendy who □ □
□ wendy heck are you going to let me in □ □ said biff □
□ ha ha ha □ □ laughed bessie □

the patient said □ □ doctor □ doctor □ I keep thinking I □ m a fly □ □
□ well □ buzz off □ □ said the doctor □

Name ______________________ Date ______________

Revision

1 In the jokes below the boxes show where punctuation marks have been missed out. Write the correct **punctuation mark** in each box. Put in all the **capital letters.**

□ knock □ knock □ □ said biff □
□ who □ s there □ □ asked bessie □ with a grin □
□ dummy □ □ answered biff □
bessie asked □ □ dummy who □ □
□ dummy a favour and let me come in □ □ said biff □
□ ha ha ha □ □ laughed bessie □

the patient said □ □ doctor □ doctor □ I keep thinking
I □ m a hen □
□ why haven't you been to see me before □ □ asked the doctor □
□ we needed the eggs □ □ the patient replied □

2 Write out this joke again, putting in all the **capital letters** and the **punctuation marks** (where there are circles).

○ how did you get that great big bump on your head ○
david ○ ○ asked the teacher ○
○ a tomato fell on it ○ ○ answered david ○
○ but tomatoes are soft ○ ○ said the teacher ○
○ this one was in a tin ○ ○ said david ○

____

____

____

____

____

Name ______________________ Date ____________

Revision

1 Read this play carefully. The boxes show where **punctuation marks** are missing. Put in all the **capital letters** and write the correct **punctuation mark** in each box.

Full stop **.** Question mark **?** Exclamation mark **!**
Comma **,** Apostrophe **'**

Hansel	look at this lovely little cottage □
Gretel	it □ s all made of sweets and cakes □
Hansel	there are lollies □ fruit drops □ marzipan and liquorice allsorts □
Gretel	there are fairy cakes □ swiss rolls □ fruit scones and chocolate crispies □
Hansel	what a wonderful house □
Gretel	who do you think lives in it □

The witch comes to the door □

Witch	I do □
Hansel	gosh □ good morning □ miss □
Witch	and who might you be □ wandering in my woods □
Hansel	we □ re called hansel and gretel □ we □ re lost □ and we □ re trying to find our way home □
Witch	why don □ t you come into my house and have a rest □
Gretel	dad said we should never go into a stranger □ s house □

2 Put in the missing **punctuation** and **capital letters**.

Witch	I m not a stranger it s you who are the strangers round here
Hansel	I m sure we d be safe in this lady s house
Witch	of course you will
Gretel	all right then
Hansel	can I have a lolly
Witch	of course you can

Name ______________________________ Date ______________

Revision

1 Read this play carefully. The boxes show where **punctuation marks** are missing. Put in all the **capital letters** and write the correct **punctuation mark** in each box.

Full stop **.** Question mark **?** Exclamation mark **!**
Comma **,** Apostrophe **'**

Cinderella	oh ☐ I wish I could go to the ball ☐
Fairy godmother	how unhappy you sound ☐ my dear ☐
Cinderella	who are you ☐ where did you come from ☐
Fairy godmother	I am your fairy godmother and I have appeared from nowhere to help you ☐
Cinderella	gosh ☐
Fairy godmother	what exactly is the problem ☐
Cinderella	it ☐ s my ugly sisters ☐ they ☐ re cruel ☐ and mean and they make me do all the housework ☐
Fairy godmother	they sound very nasty indeed ☐
Cinderella	they are nasty ☐ they won ☐ t let me go to the prince ☐ s ball tonight ☐ everyone will be there but I have to stay at home with the washing up ☐

2 Put in the missing **punctuation** and **capital letters**.

Fairy godmother	you shall go to the ball my dear I shall need a few things to help with my spell do you have some mice some string a large rat and a pumpkin
Cinderella	I suppose I could get them
Fairy godmother	then hurry up the ball will be starting soon

Name ______________________________ Date ____________

Revision

1 Read this story carefully. The boxes show where **punctuation marks** are missing. Put in all the **capital letters** and write the correct **punctuation mark** in each box.

Full stop **.** Question mark **?** Exclamation mark **!**
Comma **,** Apostrophe **’**

once upon a time there was a boy named jack ☐he lived in a little cottage with his mother ☐they were very poor ☐all they had was a little garden to grow food and an old cow called daisy to give them milk ☐one day things were so bad that jack ☐s mother told him to take daisy to the market and sell her so they could buy food ☐

jack set off with daisy ☐on the way they met a stranger ☐
☐ where are you going ☐☐ the stranger asked ☐
☐ I ☐m taking daisy to market to sell her ☐☐ said jack ☐
☐ I ☐m looking for a cow ☐☐ said the stranger ☐
☐ how much will you pay for her ☐☐ asked jack ☐
☐ well ☐I don ☐t have any money but you can have these magic beans ☐☐ said the stranger ☐he showed jack a bag of beans ☐
there were blue beans ☐red beans ☐yellow beans and silver beans ☐

2 Put in the missing **punctuation** and **capital letters**.

so jack sold the cow for a bag of magic beans and rushed home to show his mother she was not very pleased
you stupid boy now we have no cow and nothing to eat
she yelled
she grabbed the beans and threw them out of the window
then she sent jack to bed and sat crying until late into the night

Name ______________________________ Date ______________

Revision

1 Read this story carefully. The boxes show where **punctuation marks** are missing. Put in all the **capital letters** and write the correct **punctuation mark** in each box.

Full stop **.** Question mark **?** Exclamation mark **!**
Comma **,** Apostrophe **'**

once upon a time there was a little girl called red riding hood □ one day red riding hood □ s mother asked her to take a basket of food to grandmother □ s house in the middle of the woods □

she set off through the woods with a basket of delicious food □ her mother had packed new-laid eggs □ fresh-baked bread □ home-made jam and a sponge cake for grandmother □ s tea □

as she skipped through the woods □ red riding hood had the feeling that someone was watching her □ she was right □ a big bad wolf lived in the woods and he was very interested in the little girl □ suddenly he jumped out from behind a tree □
□ good morning □ □ said the wolf □
□ good morning □ □ said red riding hood □ rather nervously □
□ where are you off to this fine morning □ □ asked the wolf □
□ I □ m going to my grandmother □ s house on the other side of the wood □ □ answered red riding hood □
□ I see □ □ said the wolf □ smiling as he went on his way □

2 Put in the missing **punctuation** and **capital letters**.

little red riding hood continued on her walk through the woods she didn t know that the wolf had taken a short cut to her grandmother s house forced his way in and shut grandmother in a cupboard by the time red riding hood arrived the wolf dressed in grandmother s clothes was lying in bed waiting for her

Name ______________________________ Date ______________

Revision

1 Read this play carefully, working out where the punctuation should go. Rewrite it, putting in the missing **capital letters** and **punctuation marks**.

Full stop **.** Question mark **?** Exclamation mark **!**
Comma **,** Apostrophe **'**

jane	I dont want to go to school today
mum	why ever not
jane	everybody hates me
mum	no they dont
jane	I dont like school dinners
mum	nonsense school dinners are lovely
jane	the work is too hard for me
mum	dont be silly you can do it easily you must go to school whether you like it or not
jane	why
mum	because youre the head teacher

Name ______________________ Date ____________

Revision

1 Read this play carefully, working out where the punctuation should go. Rewrite it, putting in the missing **capital letters** and **punctuation marks**.

Full stop **.** Question mark **?** Exclamation mark **!**
Comma **,** Apostrophe **'**

Doctor	next patient please
Mr Sims	hello doctor
Doctor	goodness gracious mr sims what is the matter with your nose
Mr Sims	it hurts
Doctor	Im sure it does it looks very sore indeed how did it get like that
Mr Sims	it happened when I sniffed a brose in my friends back garden
Doctor	dont you mean a rose
Mr Sims	thats right
Doctor	but theres no b in rose
Mr Sims	there was in this one

Name ______________________ Date ____________

Revision

1 Read this story carefully, and sort out who is speaking at each point. Then rewrite it, starting a new line when someone new starts to speak and putting in all the **capital letters** and **punctuation marks**.

Full stop **.** Question mark **?** Exclamation mark **!**
Speech marks **“ ”** Comma **,** Apostrophe **’**

one night mum was tucking rosie up in bed have you said your prayers she asked yes Ive said a great big prayer tonight replied rosie gosh what was it about asked mum well I asked god to make four and four make nine from now on said rosie why do you want him to do that asked mum because thats what I put in my maths test this afternoon said rosie

Name ______________________ Date ____________

Revision

1 Read this story carefully, and sort out who is speaking at each point. Then rewrite it, starting a new line when someone new starts to speak and putting in all the **capital letters** and **punctuation marks**.

Full stop **.** Question mark **?** Exclamation mark **!**

Speech marks **“ ”** Comma **,** Apostrophe **’**

one day tom and rosie were chatting on their way home from school it was going to be their mums birthday on saturday have you got mum a present yet asked tom yes ive got her a food mixer answered rosie tom was amazed wasn t that rather expensive he asked oh no it was quite cheap really said rosie and she took the present out of her bag it was a wooden spoon

Name ______________________ Date ____________

Revision

1 Read this story carefully, and sort out who is speaking at each point. Then rewrite it, starting a new line when someone new starts to speak and putting in all the **capital letters** and **punctuation marks**.

Full stop **.** Question mark **?** Exclamation mark **!**
Speech marks **“ ”** Comma **,** Apostrophe **’**

the phone rang at coppit primary school hello said the headteacher hello said a hoarse voice on the other end of the phone what can I do for you the headteacher asked I m just ringing to say that sam bloggs wont be in school today said the voice is he ill asked the headteacher yes he has bad flu and he s got to stay in bed replied the voice who is that speaking please asked the headteacher there was a pause and then the voice replied this is my father